Business
Widows

A Note About the Author

In between producing books such as *Business Widows* and its predecessors, *Golf Widows* and *Cricket Widows*, Noel Ford is a regular contributor to many magazines and newspapers; from *Punch* and *Private Eye* through to the *Church Times, Truck* and *Plastics & Rubber Weekly*.

When he's finished all that, he designs greetings cards and writes and illustrates the odd children's book, not to mention any advertising jobs that come his way.

Rarely seen outside his natural habitat, a high-tech garret at the top of his Leicestershire home, he sits surrounded by his three telephones, answering machine, two computers, fax machine, word processor, two printers, intercom system, copier, teletext tv and VCR.

Now that he has finished this latest project, he hopes to spend a few minutes with his wife, Margaret and daughter, Sara.

Business Widows

A HANDBOOK FOR WORKAHOLICS

NOEL FORD

ANGUS
& ROBERTSON
PUBLISHERS

AN ANGUS & ROBERTSON BOOK

Angus & Robertson (UK)
16 Golden Square, London W1R 4BN
United Kingdom and
Collins/Angus & Robertson Publishers Australia
Unit 4, Eden Park, 31 Waterloo Road,
North Ryde, NSW, Australia 2113
William Collins Publishers Ltd
31 View Road, Glenfield, Auckland 10,
New Zealand

First published in the United Kingdom by
Angus & Robertson (UK) in 1990
First published in Australia by
Collins/Angus & Robertson Publishers in 1990

Text and illustrations copyright © Noel Ford 1990

Typeset in Great Britain by AKM Associates (UK) Ltd

Printed in Great Britain by Scotprint Ltd, Musselburgh, Scotland

British Library Cataloguing in Publication Data

Ford, Noel
    Business widows: a handbook for workaholics.
    1. Business firms
    I. Title
    338.7

    ISBN 0 207 16874 1

Contents

Foreword

Throughout history, womankind has suffered many hardships and injustices. For years they have found themselves cast as second-class citizens; they have been forced to humbly submit to husbands' unreasonable demands; they have never been able to find a supermarket trolley that runs in a straight line.

True, in recent years, many wrongs have been put right (though not, alas, the supermarket trolleys) and women of the late twentieth century have acquired a status that would have been unimaginable to their forbears. Yet still, many of today's women are living in conditions with which those same forbears would sympathise. These are the women with workaholic husbands.

Throughout history? Certainly. You think Attila the Hun was mad? You should have seen the wife he left stuck at home with the kids while he was yomping all over Europe with the lads, giving the Goths and Gauls a hard time!

And what about the humble foot-soldier who gave his wife a peck on the cheek and told her he was 'just popping down the road for a bit of a scrap'? Would she have let him go so easily if he'd told her it was the Hundred Years War?

Today, scientists are frankly baffled by the phenomenon of the workaholic husband. Any other species in which the female saw so little of its mate would have died out ages ago. Far from dying out, however, the species is multiplying at a frightening rate. As fast as technology can develop better and better time and labour saving gadgets such as the fax machine and the word processor, the workaholic is developing better and better excuses to spend more time with them than with his spouse. The more . . . excuse me, I thought I heard something. Yes, I thought so. My wife, calling up the stairs.

'Are you coming to bed? It's three o'clock in the morning!'

'I'll only be a few minutes.'

'You said that two hours ago.'

'Er . . . yes. I've nearly finished. Just got to wrap up this intro for the book.'

'Book?'

'Yes, you know. *Business Widows.* It's about husbands who spend all their time working while their wives . . . er, while their wives . . .'

Oh dear, she's coming up the stairs now.

'Ah. There you are, dear. You didn't have to come up, I was just coming dow . . . What are you holding behind your back, dear? An axe? Wait a minute, no, really, I'll come right now. No. No! You can't do it! Please! Not that! Not my word proce . . . .

Working Relationships

'You say *you're my husband* . . . *do you have any official identification?*'

'I've got an assistant now, dear. I should be able
to spend more time with you and the kids . . .
how many is it we've got now?'

'It's the Old Man's idea. Reckons his young executives should see more of their families'

'I didn't tell you, did I? My wife and I are trying
for a baby . . . so, if you don't mind staying out
of this office between 2.00 and 2.05 this
afternoon . . .'

'Your wife's back again, Dennis'

'If we're going to come to grips with your
obsession with working, you have to let me take
my own notes!'

'Your wife's on the phone. You know . . . the short lady with curly brown hair and the nervous twitch'

'I was quite pleased to find a job which allows
me to see more of my husband'

*'Look, I'm half-way through a meeting, this
better be bloody important!'*

'I'm afraid I'm going to be late home for dinner
again, Mavis . . . about three days'

'More paperwork? Pile it on, pile it on . . .'

'Well, actually, it is rather urgent . . . could you
make an appointment for me to see my husband
before next Thursday?'

'Leap Years aren't so bad . . . on average I get to
see him an extra 23.61 seconds a day'

'According to my operative's report, Mrs Atkins,
your husband *does* appear to be working all the
time. He was seen, briefly, with a woman on one
occasion but he thinks that may have been you . . .'

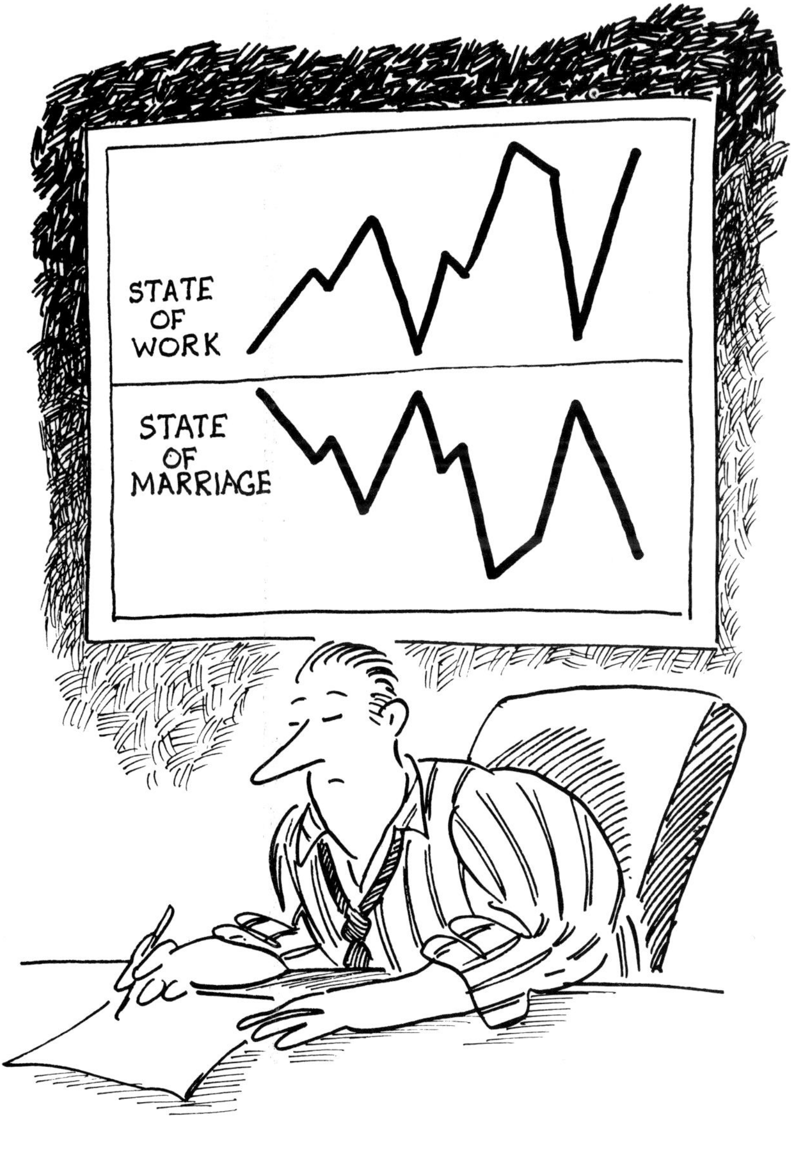
STATE
OF
WORK
STATE
OF
MARRIAGE

'Dear Sir, in reply to . . . BLOW . . . your letter
of the . . . BLOW . . . 17th inst., I am pleased . . .
BLOW . . . to inform you . . .'

'I quite understand, darling . . . there's no need
for you to stop working to be present for the
birth. After all, you didn't stop for the
conception!'

'Planning and Strategy meeting at 9.30
Appointment with clients at 10.30
Briefing with M.D. at 11.45
Working lunch at 1.00
Sales Conference at 3.00
Your wife's throwing herself under a bus at 4.00
Finance meeting at 4.15 . . .'

'Really, Muriel, must *we go through this every
time I work late at the office?*'

Hi-Technoholics

'I remember when your father used to sit me on
his lap and look at me like that'

'Talking of non-compatible peripherals, have you
seen my wife?'

'Susan! . . . are you trying to tell me we have an
interface problem?'

'Henry's at his drama class tonight . . . he feels his
telephone answering machine messages lack
dynamic projection'

'The doctor can deal with you now . . . he had to
sedate your wife to stop her laughing'

'He's fluent in twenty-four computer languages
and never says a bloody word to me'

'Nasty case . . . wife dropped his hardware onto
his software'

'Bad news, Sidney . . . your wife's hacked into the
company computer'

'. . . and another thing . . . stop referring to me as
user-friendly'

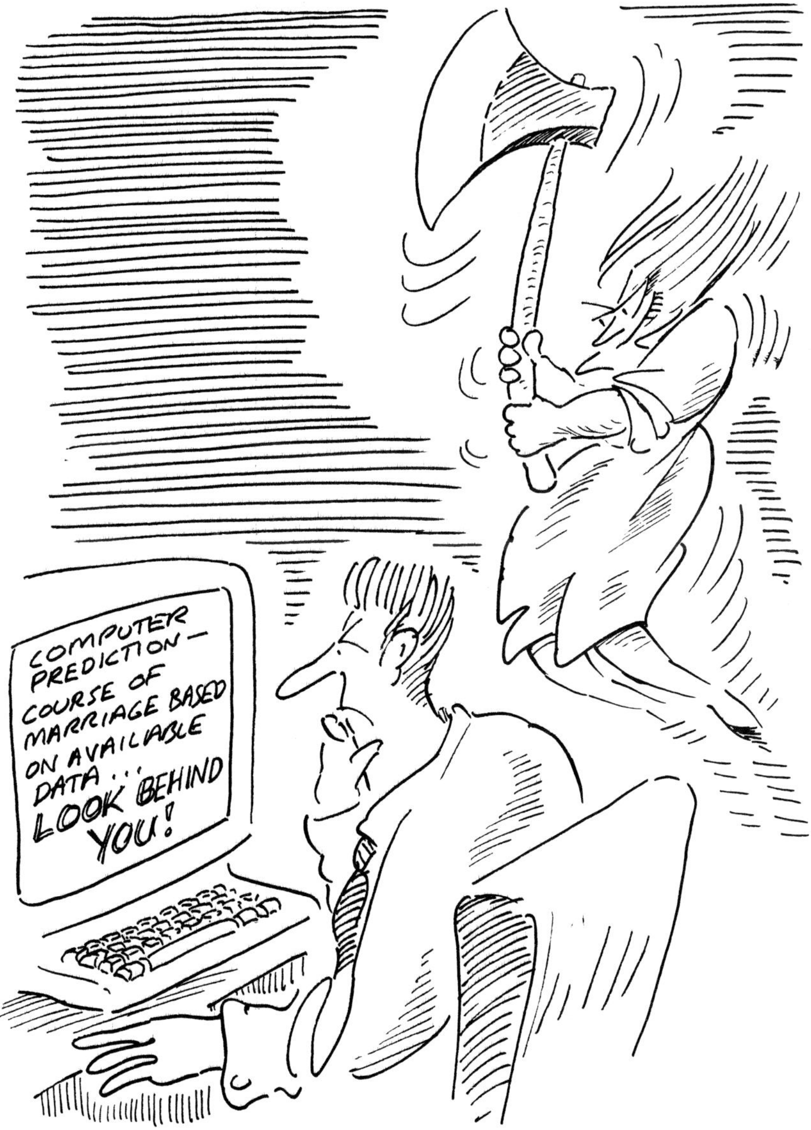
COMPUTER PREDICTION—
COURSE OF MARRIAGE BASED ON AVAILABLE DATA...
LOOK BEHIND YOU!

'George was only interested in mega-bytes, so I
got him this rottweiler . . .'

'No, officer, I can't imagine how he came to get
his foot caught in his computer printer'

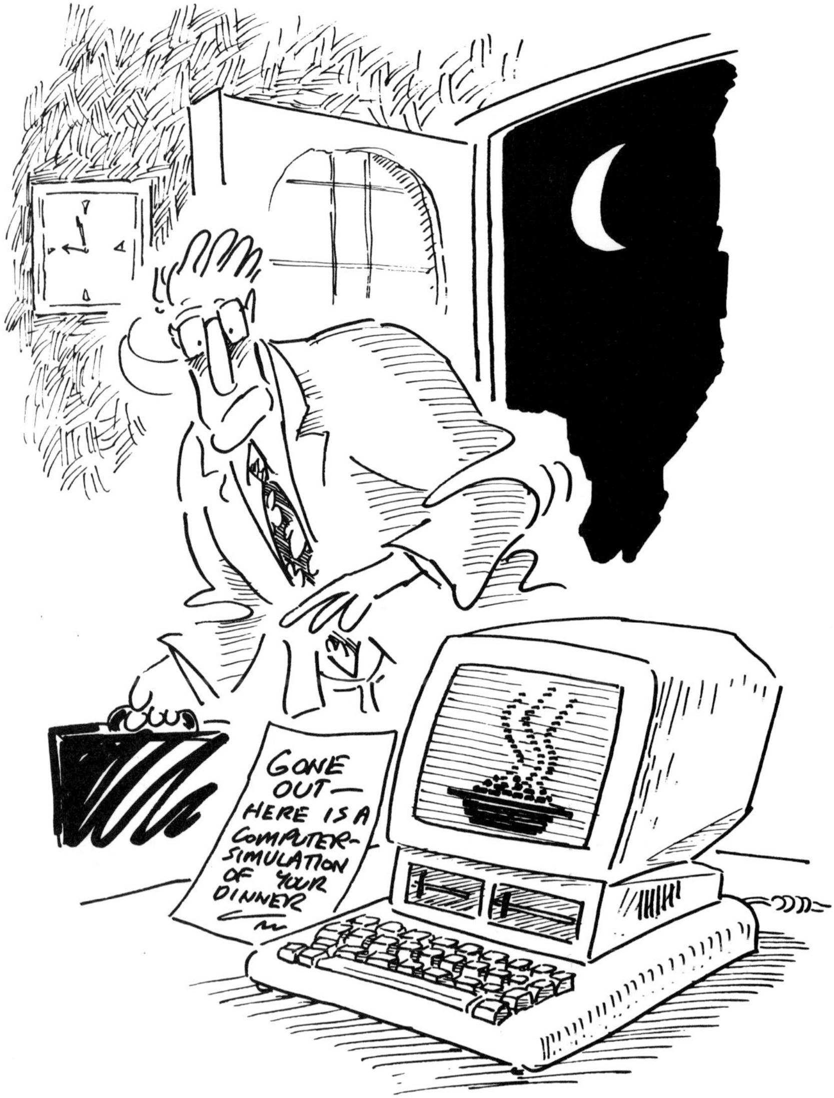
GONE OUT— HERE IS A COMPUTER-SIMULATION OF YOUR DINNER

The Workaholic on Holiday

'For goodness sake, Albert, try to remember
you're on the Orient Express this week!'

'I'm glad to see you're taking our holiday
seriously this year'

'Now will you take back everything you said
when I insisted on bringing my desk on the
cruise?'

'I wish you wouldn't keep your desk-top
calculator tucked in your swimming shorts'

'Hello, Mrs Thomas, I'm Jerry Harris from the
office. Good news! Your husband has finally
learned to delegate . . . he's asked me to take you
and the kids on holiday'

'I'm afraid there'll be an excess-baggage charge on
your Filofax'

'Take a good look, dear . . . it will probably have
fallen over completely by the next time I get you
away from the office'

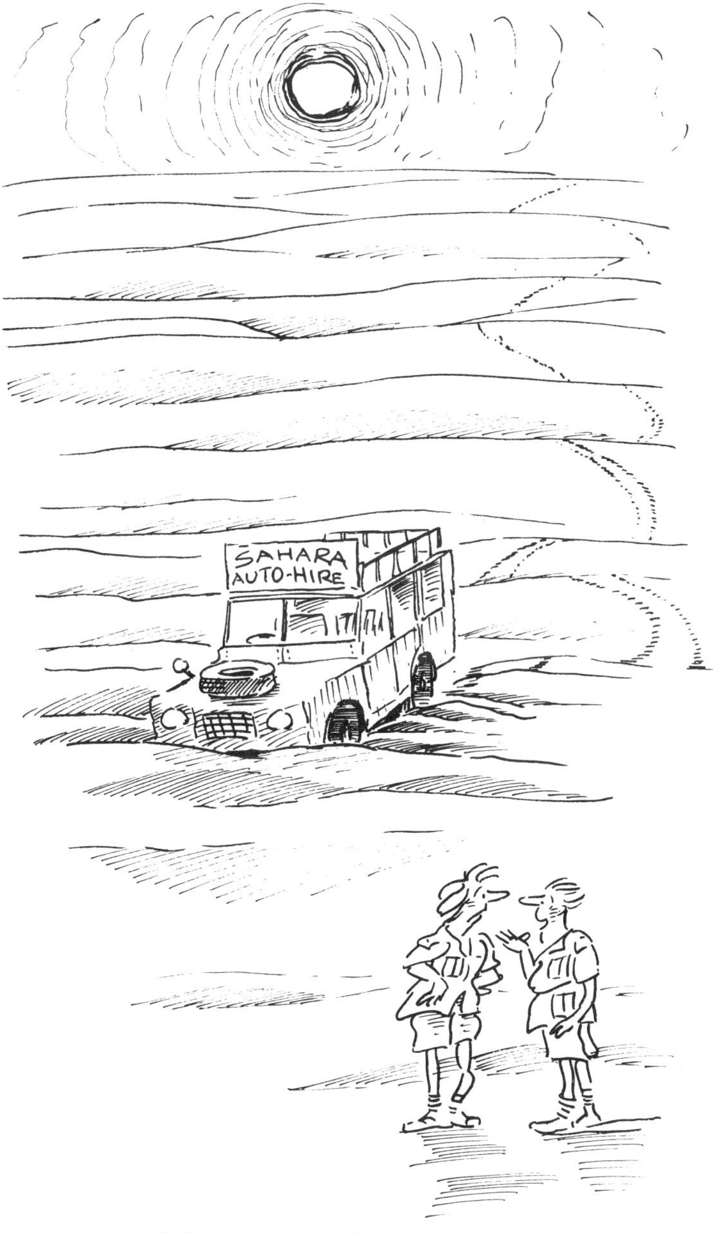
SAHARA
AUTO-HIRE

'But I did take care of the food and water, dear . . . I've brought a wallet full of Luncheon Vouchers'

'Hello dear, listen . . . I've found us the perfect
little holiday apartment . . .'

'Excuse me, dear . . . the rickshaw phone . . .'

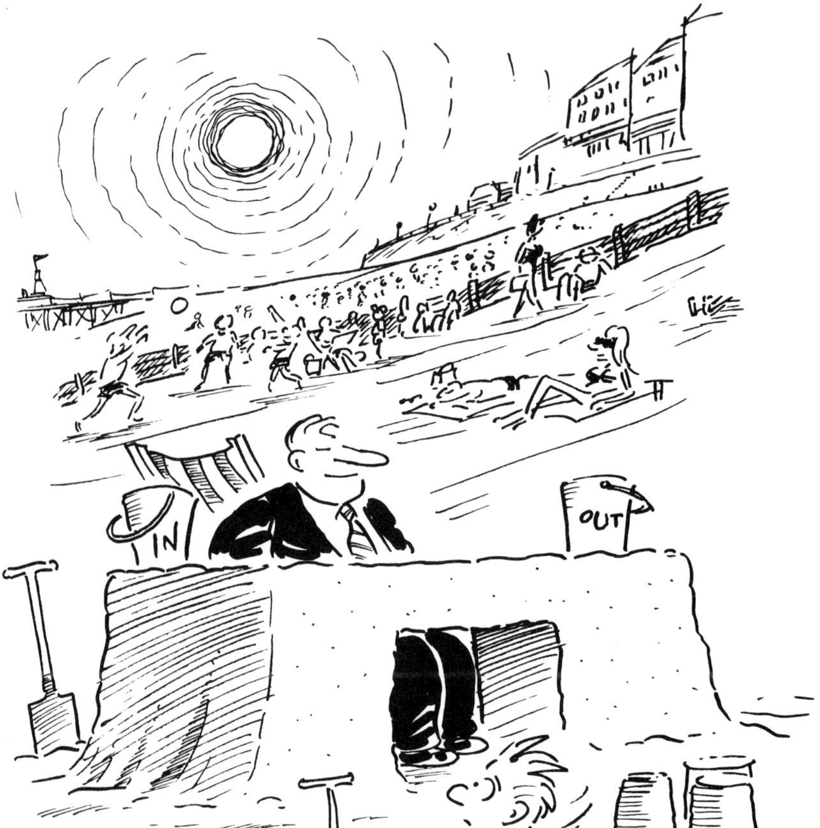
IN
OUT

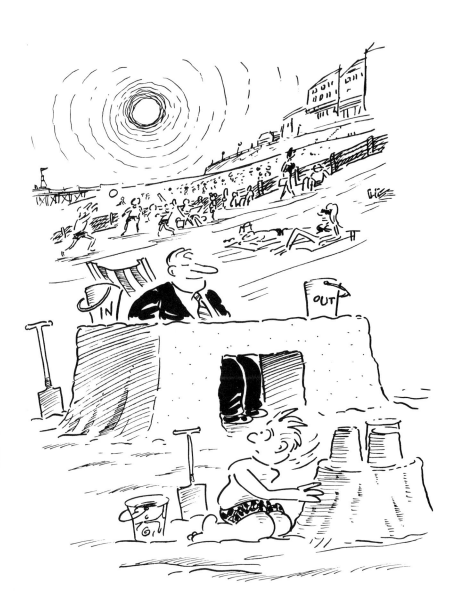

'I'm sorry, he left for his annual holiday this
morning and won't be back until late this
afternoon'

'Yes, it is true! I've finally persuaded Derek to
take a holiday'

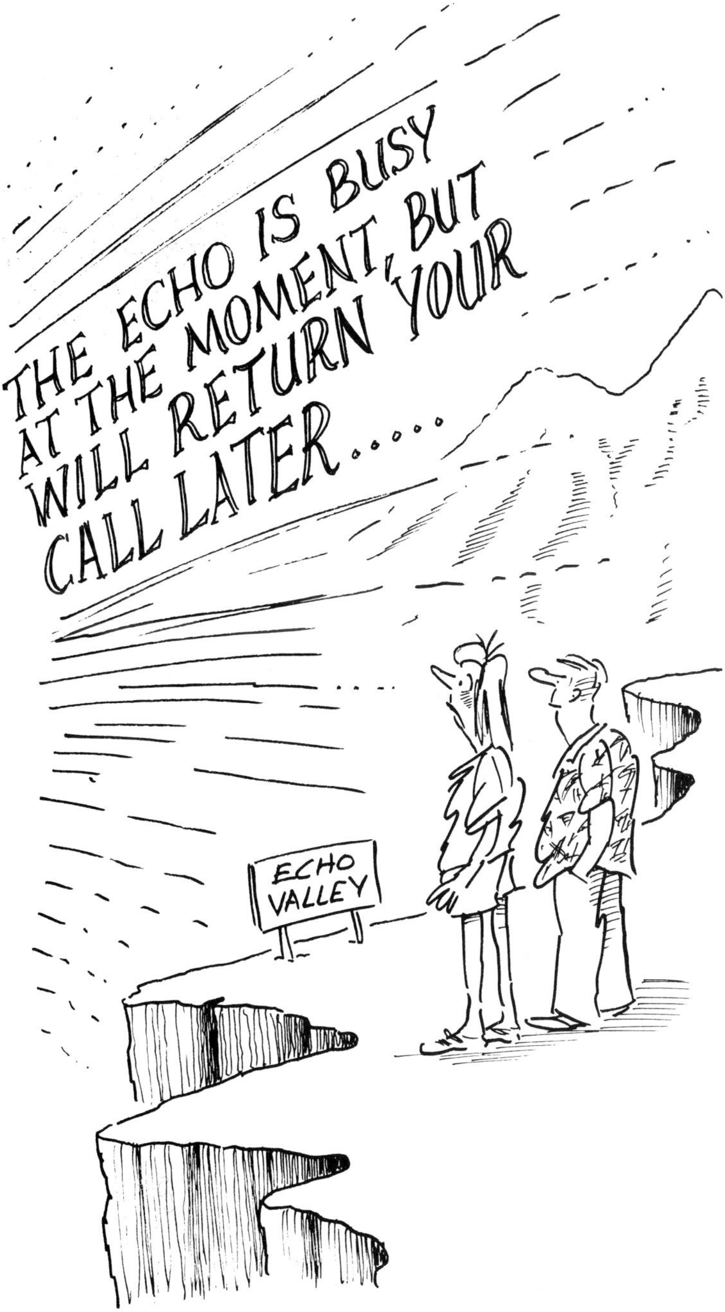
THE ECHO IS BUSY AT THE MOMENT, BUT WILL RETURN YOUR CALL LATER......
ECHO VALLEY

'Isn't he thoughtful? He never forgets to send us a
postcard when he's away on holiday'

'I'll say it's mind-boggling. To think . . . the
wives of the blokes who built that probably saw
even less of their husbands than we do'

'Do get a move on, darling . . . my filing cabinet
isn't that heavy'

'I knew it was too much to hope that we'd found
a holiday spot where your father couldn't possibly
run into a business acquaintance'

'Did you have to bring your damned secretary?'

Termination
of Contract

'Yes, I do have an appointment. I believe his wife
arranged it'

'Talking of contracts, darling, I've just signed one
myself'

'Hello again, Marlene . . . they're letting me
commute'

'I do believe he's finally stopped working . . . at
least, he's not answering his phone'

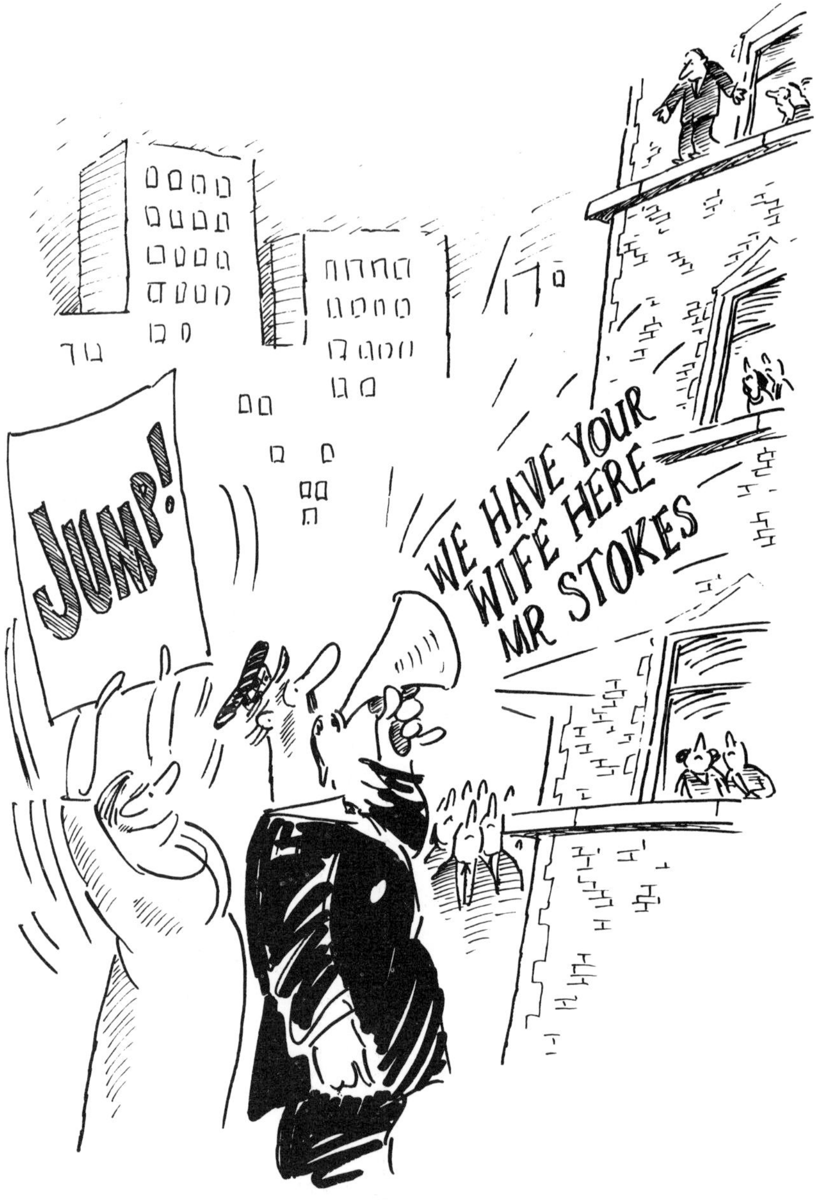
JUMP!
WE HAVE YOUR
WIFE HERE
MR STOKES

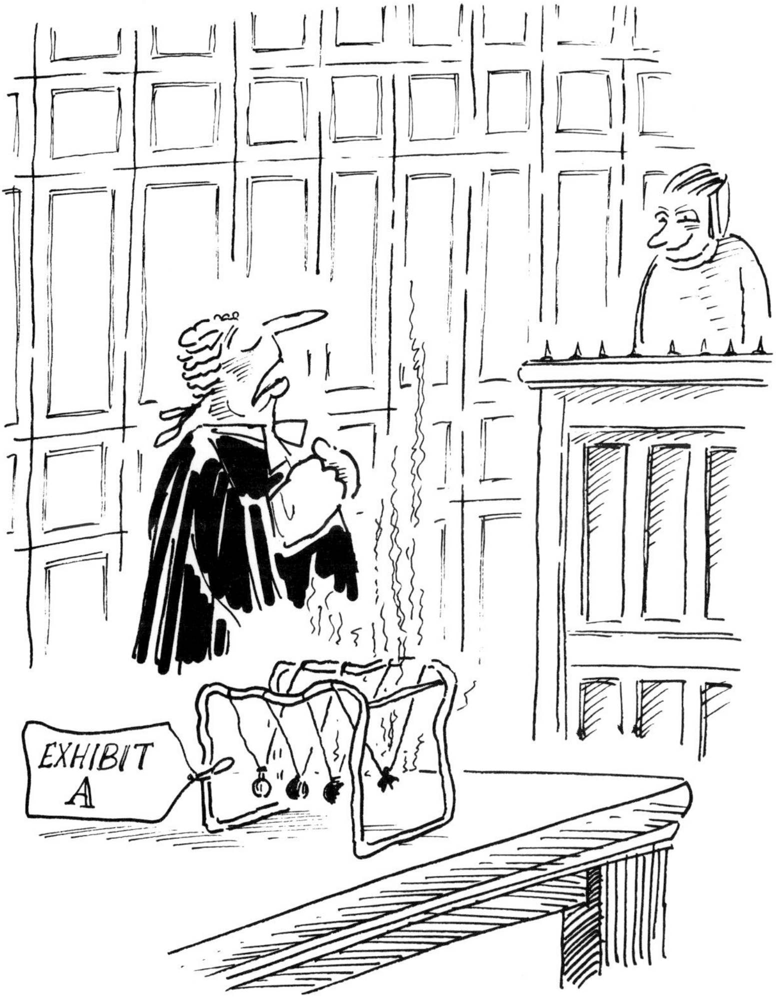
EXHIBIT
A

'So, you don't deny putting plastic explosive in your husband's executive toy?'

'Hello, I fear Mr Johnson will be rather late into
the office today . . . he's in a meeting'

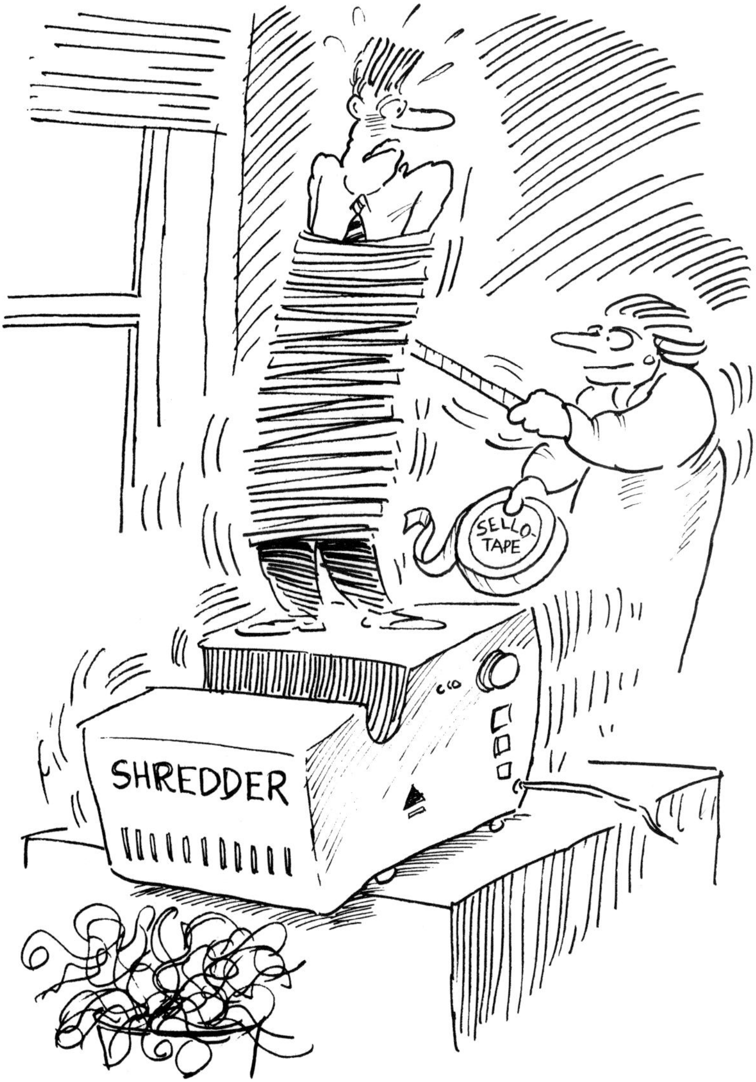
SELLO-
TAPE
SHREDDER

'Can't we talk this over?'

'You have to hand it to his wife. She's found a
sure-fire way to get him away from the office on
time'

'Mind you, Alfred did teach me the importance of
keeping things neatly filed in their place'

Questionnaire

'Should I divorce my workaholic husband?'
Discover the answer to this important question by completing The Business Widows' Decision-Maker Questionnaire.

Key: No '✳✳✳' answers: ---Admit it! The moment you picked up your pen to do this test, your husband snatched it from your hand and insisted on doing the paperwork for you. So, yes, divorce him.

Between one and five '✳✳✳' answers: ---There is a chance that your marriage can be saved. Bookmakers are quoting it at around five-thousand-to one so, yes, divorce him.

More than five '✳✳✳' answers: ---You can divorce him if you like but, honestly, you won't notice any difference.

Your husband never goes anywhere without his portable telephone because . . .

✳   He can't bear to be out of touch with you.

✳✳   He can't bear to be out of touch with clients.

✳✳✳   You have stuffed it somewhere even modern surgical techniques cannot reach.

BEEEEEEP
BEEEEEP

In the middle of an important meeting, your husband realises that he has left some crucial papers at home. He phones and asks you to fax them to him from . . .

*   The Fax Bureau down the road.

**   The fax machine in his study.

***   The fax machine in the bathroom as this is closer than the fax machines in the study, living room, bedroom, kitchen, garden shed . . .

When you ask him which comes first, his office or his home, your husband replies? . . .

*   'My home.'

**   'My office.'

***   'What's the difference?'

Your husband is late home every night. You suspect he may be having an affair and you ask him if this is the case. He replies . . .

✳   'It's a fair cop.'   ✳✳   'I'm much too busy for that sort of thing!'

✳✳✳   'Just a moment, I'll have to ask my secretary'

On your birthday, your husband always sends you . . .

*   A big bunch of roses.   **   A birthday card.

***   A memo.

Your husband gets most of his meals and drinks from vending-machines because . . .

*   It gives him more time for work.

**   The meals you make for him are always cold by the time he gets home.

***   He's converted your kitchen into a home office.

Your husband only sleeps four hours a night because . . .

*   That's all he needs.

**   That's all he has time for.

***   His desk isn't all that comfortable.

In a weak moment, your husband whisks you off to Paris for a second honeymoon but, as you snuggle up to him in the luxurious Bridal Suite's double-bed, the telephone rings. He picks up the phone and says . . .

* 'I'm sorry, you must have the wrong number.'

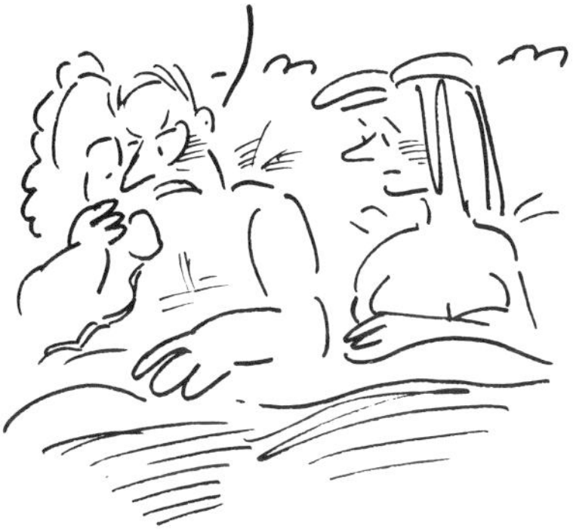

** 'I'm sorry, I'm in a meeting. Call me back in five minutes.'

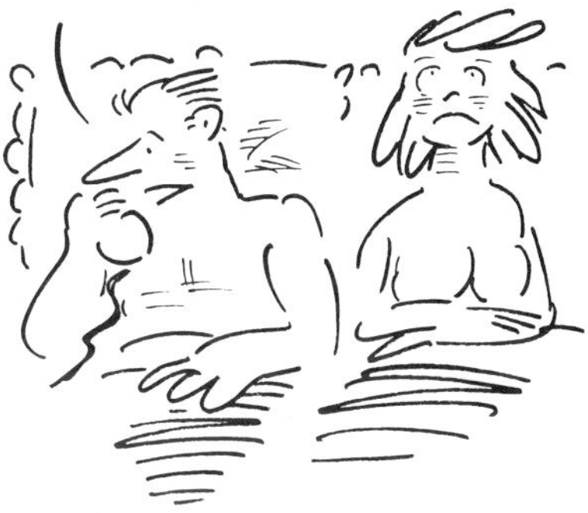

*** 'Leave the dictation for now, Janice, and take this call, please.'

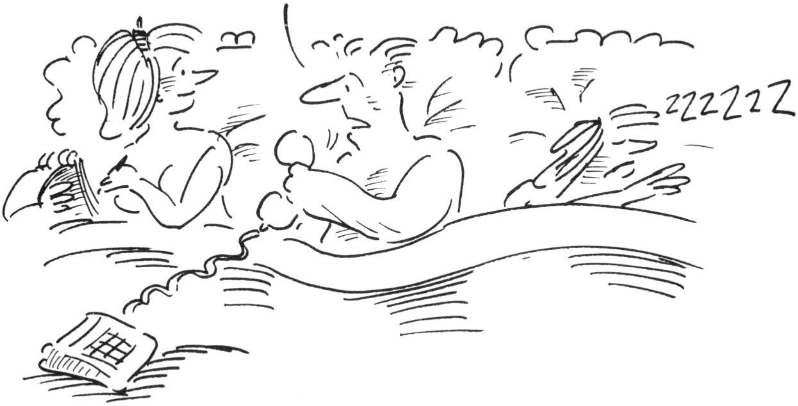
ZZZZZZ

Whilst your husband is away on business, your house burns down. When you break the news to him on the telephone, he exclaims . . .

*   'How awful!---are you all right---I'll come back at once.'

**   'How inconvenient!---are those papers I left there all right?---I'll come back tomorrow.'

***   'How could you do it?
And on our honeymoon, too!'

You have bought a dog for your husband in the hope that it will give him something other than his work to think about. He is delighted and decides to keep it . . .

✻   At home to bring his pipe and slippers.

✻✻   At work to bring his briefcase and filofax.

✻✻✻   Filed under 'D'.

In his office, your husband keeps your picture . . .

*   On his desk.   **   On his desk, behind the picture of his boss.

***   Under his desk to stop it wobbling and making the picture of his boss fall over.

The doctor tells your husband that if he doesn't slow down he'll be heading for a coronary. He replies . . .

* 'I never realised! I'll take the family on a long holiday.'

** 'Well. I suppose I could stop working every Sunday.'

*** 'A coronary?---let me see, I could just about fit one in around September, next year.'

The last time your husband said, 'I love you' was . . .

*   On your birthday.

**   On your anniversary.

***   To his Company Chairman.

After a hard day at the office, your husband likes nothing better than . . .

*   A nice relaxing evening at home.

**   A nice working evening at home.

***   A hard day at the office.

Your husband's idea of a holiday is . . .

✻   Two weeks away from it all.

✻✻   One week at a Conference Centre

✻✻✻   Paddling naked in the sea, building sand-castles and making himself sick from too much ice-cream. (Because that's what it was like when he last took a holiday!)

The last time you threatened to leave him, your husband . . .

✢   Pleaded with you not to go.

✢✢   Pleaded with you not to go until you'd finished his typing.

✢✢✢   Thought that, with your single-bed out of the way he could squeeze in a computer work-station.

When he dies, your husband would like to be . . .

❋ Buried ❋❋ Cremated ❋❋❋ Stuffed

Business Widows Hit Back

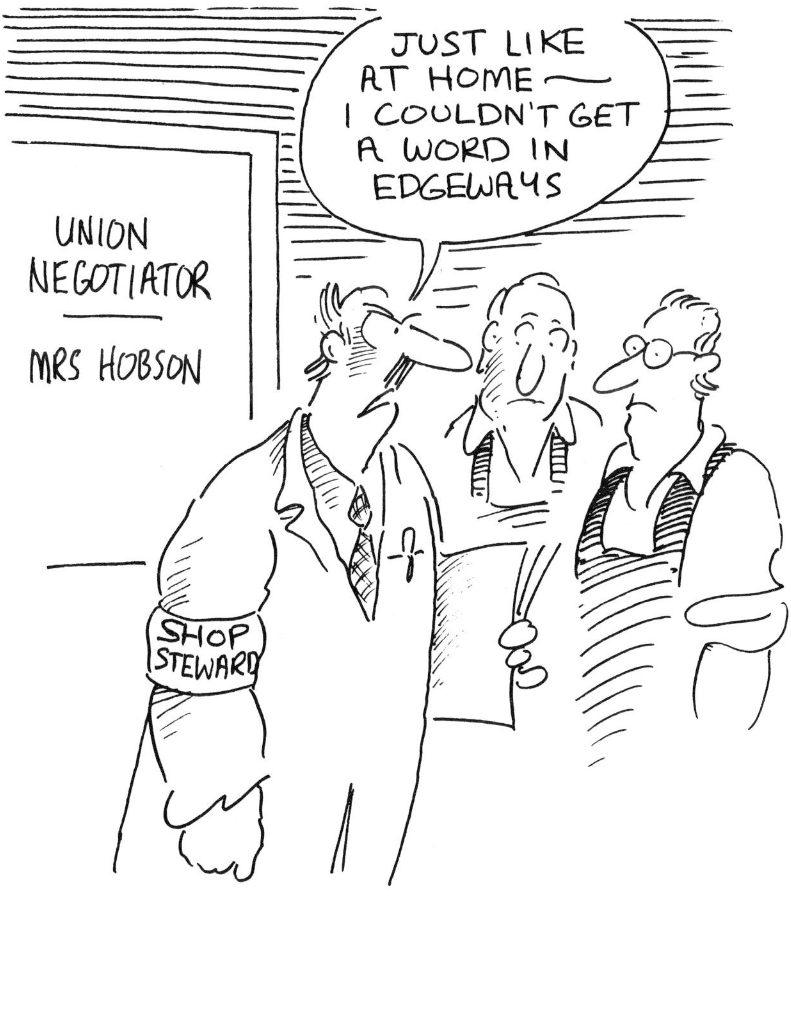
JUST LIKE AT HOME — I COULDN'T GET A WORD IN EDGEWAYS
UNION NEGOTIATOR
MRS HOBSON
SHOP STEWARD

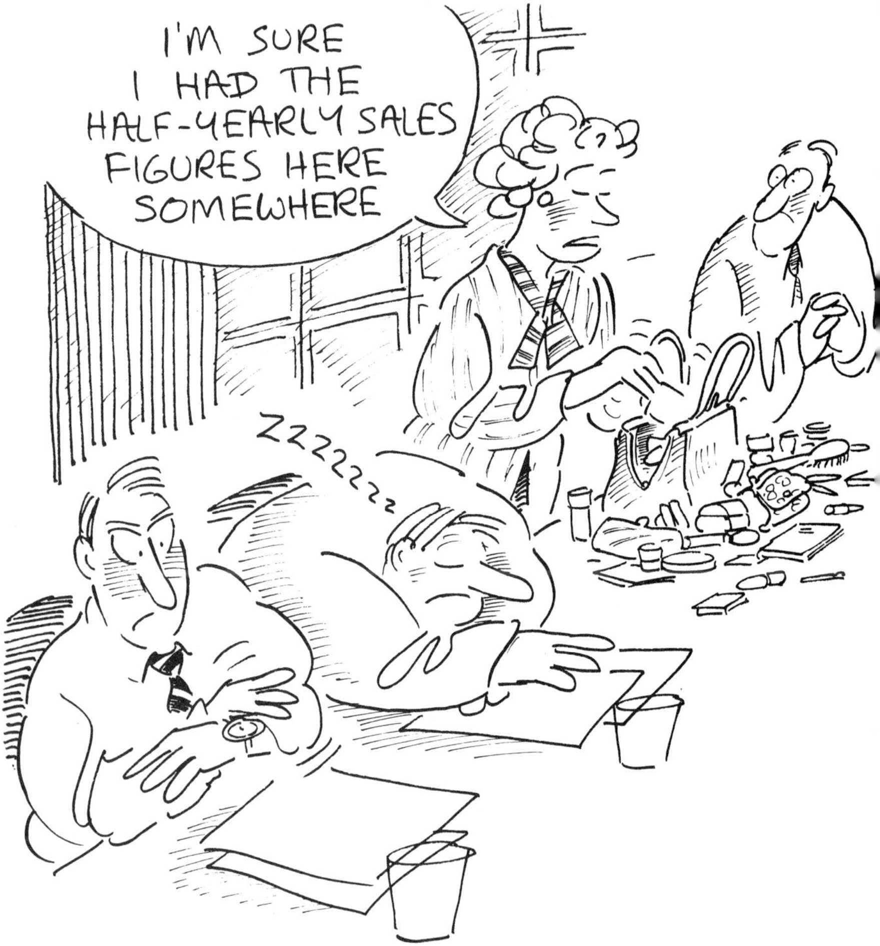
I'M SURE I HAD THE HALF-YEARLY SALES FIGURES HERE SOMEWHERE
ZZZZZZZZZ

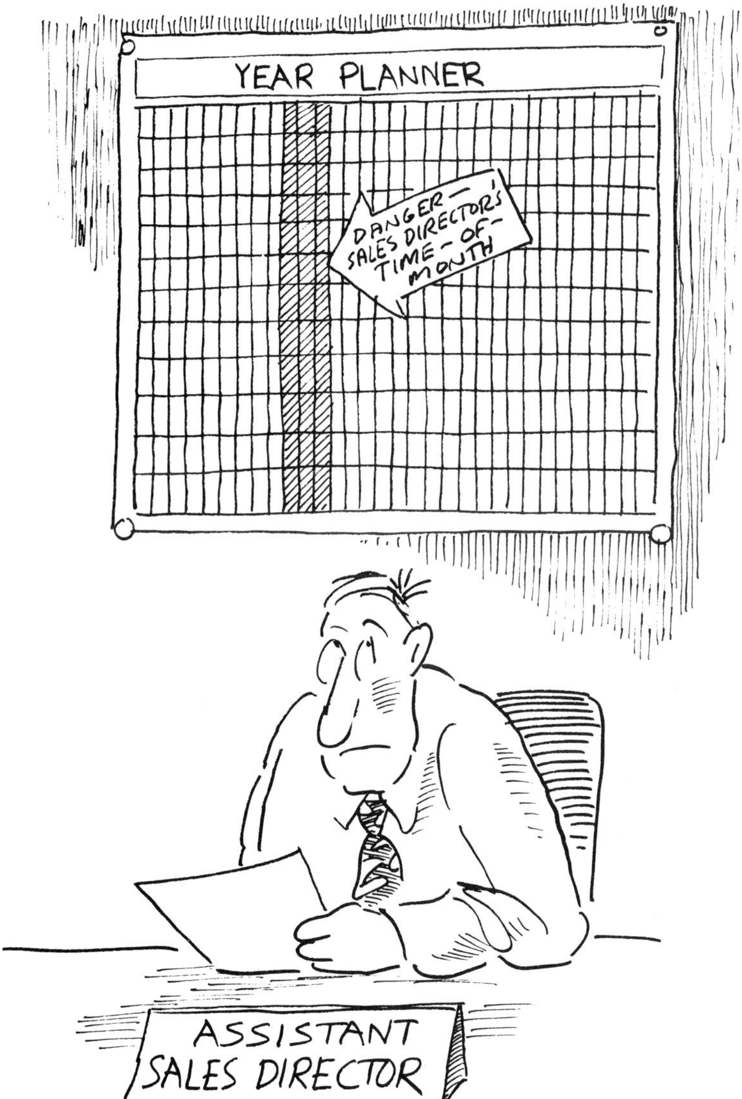
YEAR PLANNER
DANGER — SALES DIRECTOR'S TIME-OF-MONTH
ASSISTANT SALES DIRECTOR

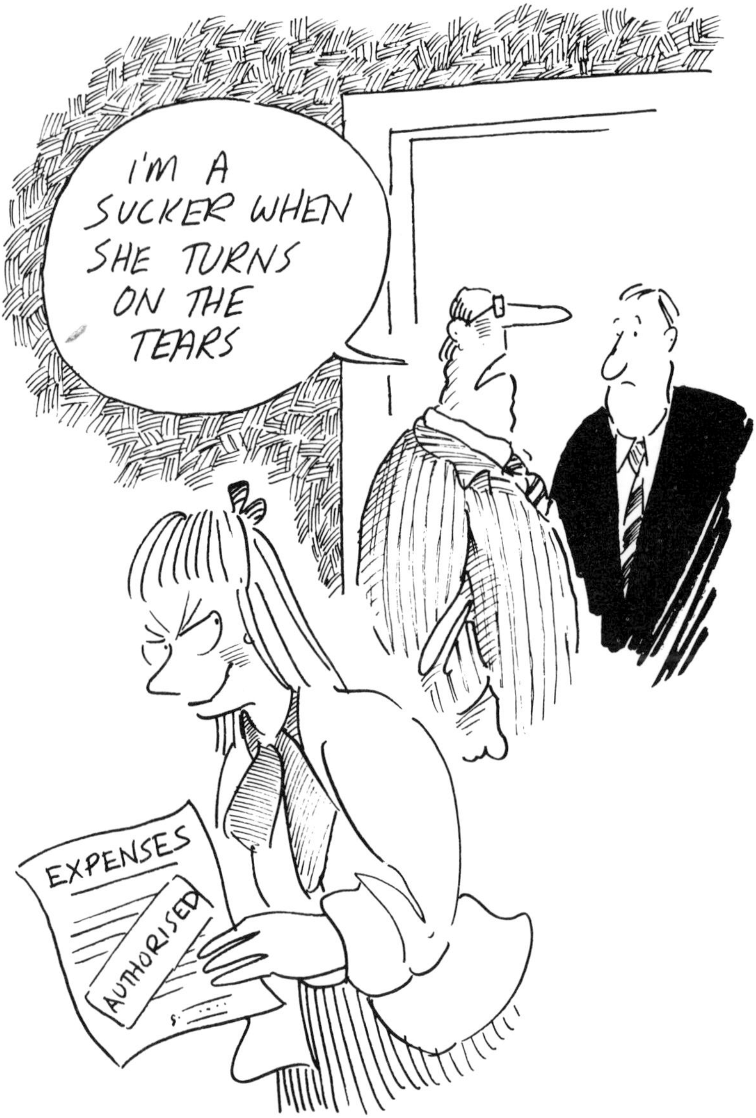
I'M A SUCKER WHEN SHE TURNS ON THE TEARS
EXPENSES
AUTHORISED

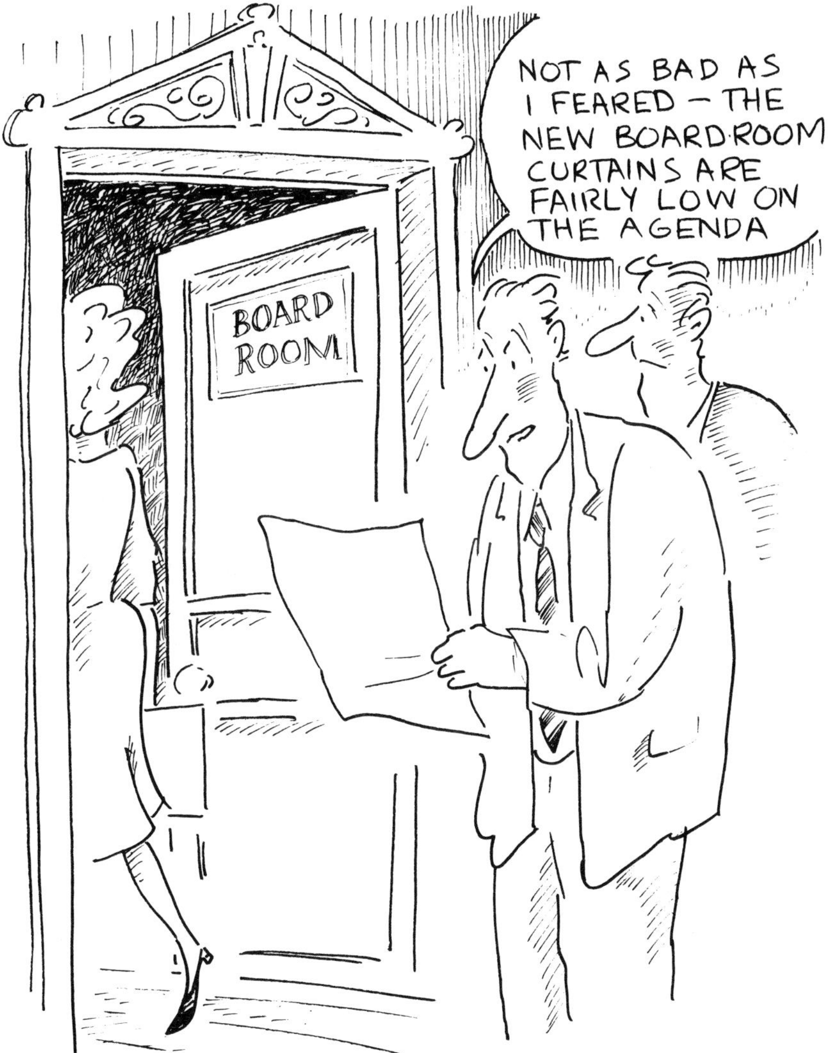
BOARD ROOM
NOT AS BAD AS I FEARED – THE NEW BOARD·ROOM CURTAINS ARE FAIRLY LOW ON THE AGENDA

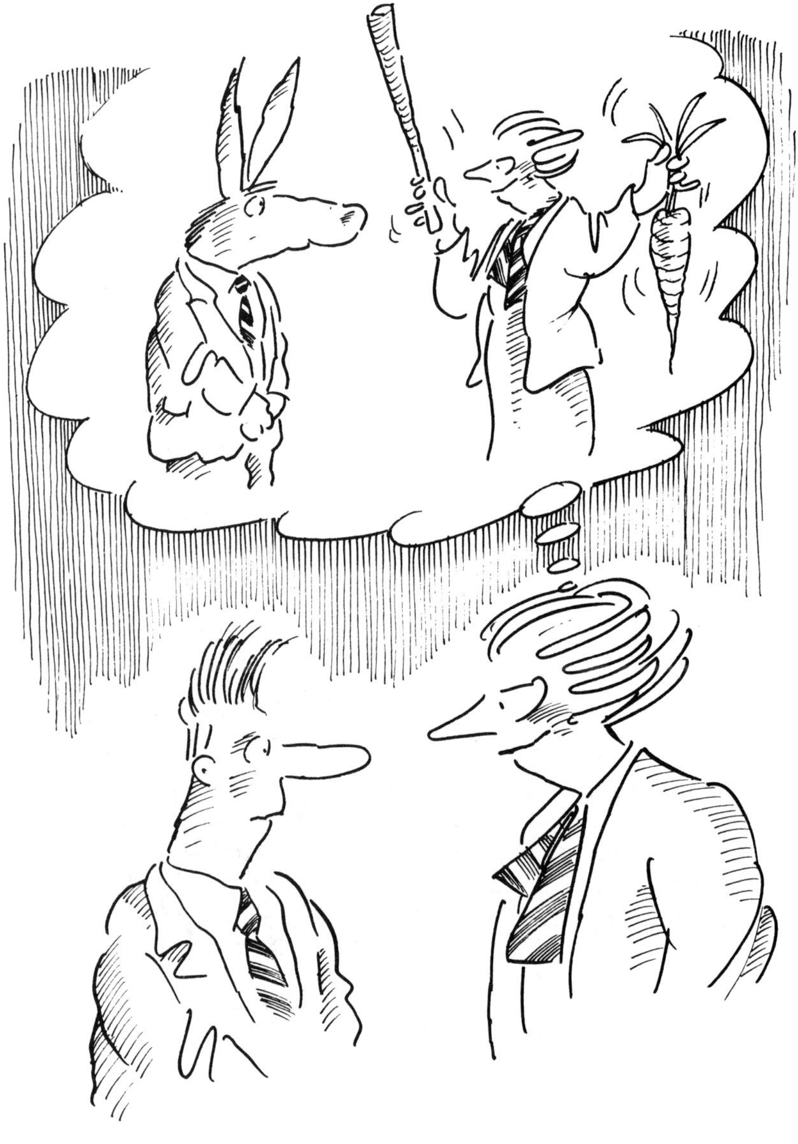

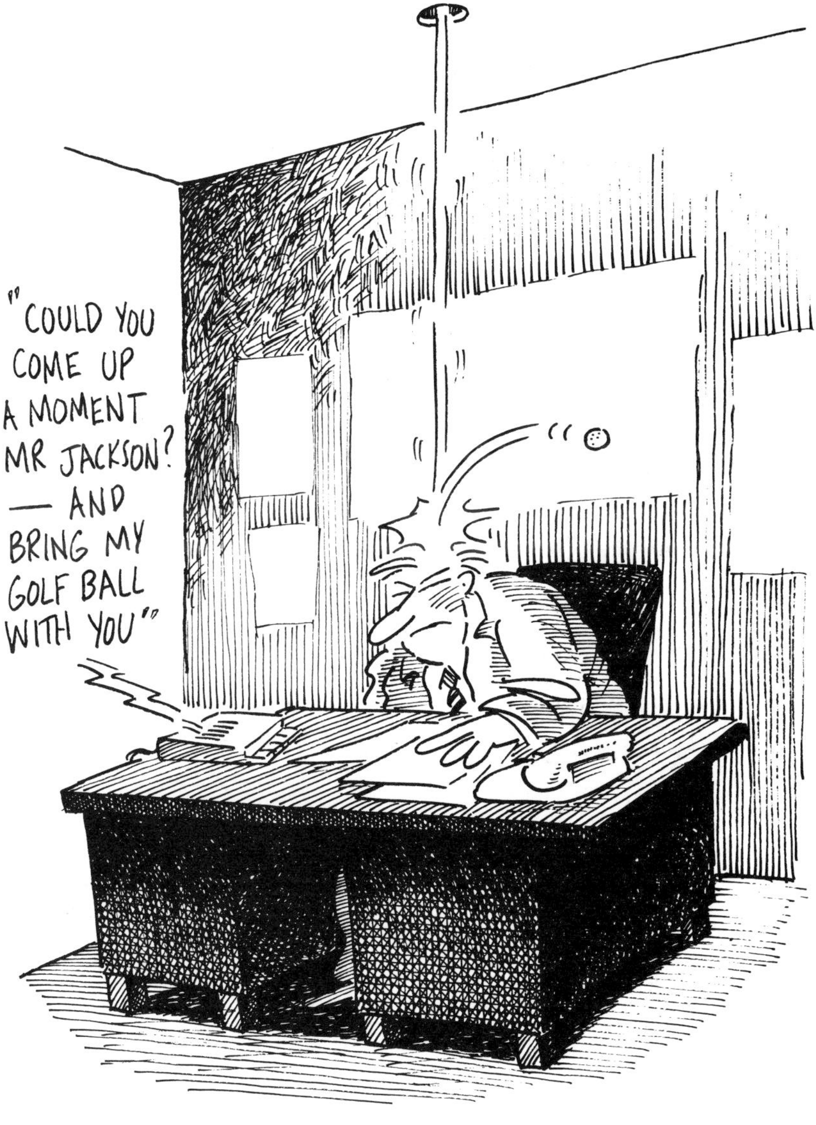
"COULD YOU COME UP A MOMENT MR JACKSON? — AND BRING MY GOLF BALL WITH YOU"

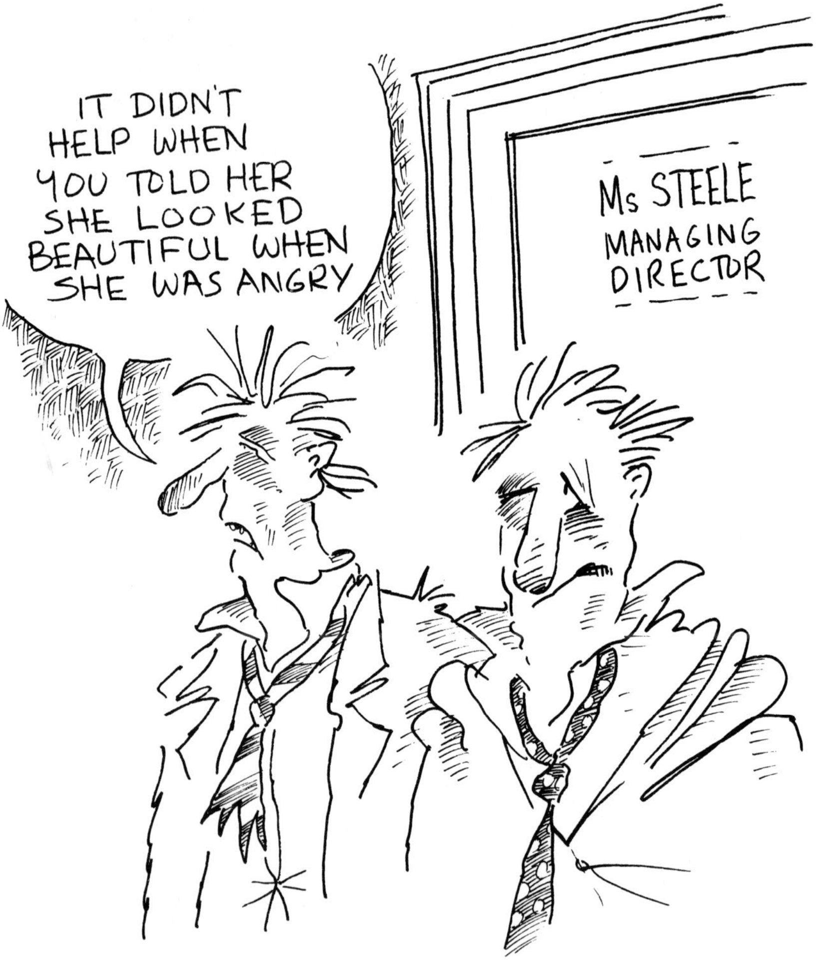
IT DIDN'T HELP WHEN YOU TOLD HER SHE LOOKED BEAUTIFUL WHEN SHE WAS ANGRY
Ms STEELE
MANAGING DIRECTOR

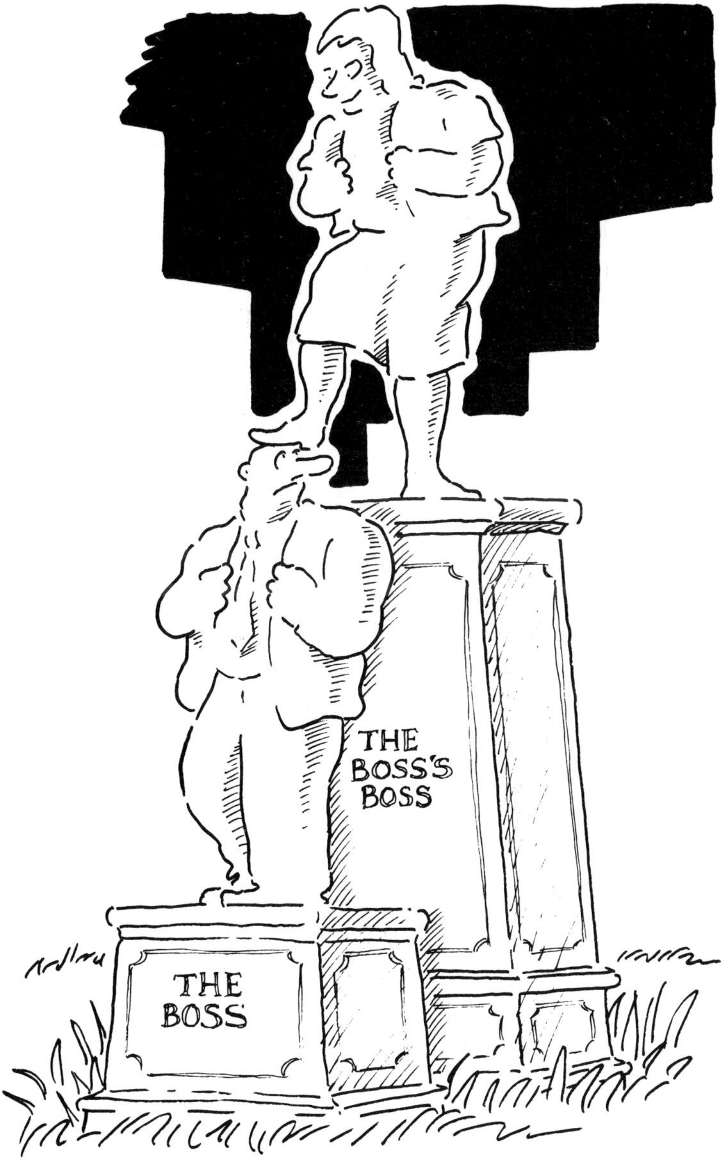
THE BOSS'S BOSS
THE BOSS